GUITAR FOR BEGINNERS

LANCE VOIGHT

GUITAR FOR BEGINNERS

How You Can Confidently Play Guitar In 10 Days, Even If You've Never Played a Single Chord In Your Life

GUITAR FOR BEGINNERS

Written By
Lance Voight

© Copyright 2019 by Lance Voight - All rights reserved.

The follow eBook is reproduced below with the goal of providing information that is as accurate and reliable as possible. Regardless, purchasing this eBook can be seen as consent to the fact that both the publisher and the author of this book are in no way experts on the topics discussed within and that any recommendations or suggestions that are made herein are for entertainment purposes only. Professionals should be consulted as needed prior to undertaking any of the action endorsed herein.

This declaration is deemed fair and valid by both the American Bar Association and the Committee of Publishers Association and is legally binding throughout the United States.

Furthermore, the transmission, duplication or reproduction of any of the following work including specific information will be considered an illegal act irrespective of if it is done electronically or in print. This extends to creating a secondary or tertiary copy of the work or a recorded copy and is only allowed with express written consent from the Publisher. All additional right reserved.

The information in the following pages is broadly considered to be a truthful and accurate account of facts and as such any inattention, use or misuse of the information in question by the reader will render any resulting actions solely under their purview. There are no scenarios in which the publisher or the original author of this work can be in any fashion deemed liable for any hardship or damages that may befall them after undertaking information described herein.

Additionally, the information in the following pages is intended only for informational purposes and should thus be thought of as universal. As befitting its nature, it is presented without assurance regarding its prolonged validity or interim quality. Trademarks that are mentioned are done without written consent and can in no way be considered an endorsement from the trademark holder.

❦ Created with Vellum

INTRODUCTION TO THE GUITAR

Hey there,
I'm Lance - and thank you for buying this book.

A little about me, and my relationship with the guitar. For roughly ten years, I have played the guitar and I'd like to say that I've reached a pretty high level. In addition to this, I've also taught many people how to play. You see, the guitar is a beautiful instrument and it has become immensely popular for a very good reason.

It's extremely expressive, you can do a huge variety of different things on it, and it's one of the few instruments where the sky is really the limit. Many instruments only allow you to play one note at a time, or are so specialized that they're beyond the reach of the casual player to the point that you can't really play that much with them. The guitar, however, is ubiquitous enough that you can do much of anything. When it comes down to what instrument a person should learn first, I will always recommend the guitar - so by purchasing your guitar, you've already made a big step in the right direction.

The guitar is also great because in order to learn to play the guitar proficiently, you have to be able to understand what you're doing at a musical level. However, the learning curve for the guitar isn't so steep that you're always left wondering what it is that you're doing. What I mean by this is that learning to play the guitar properly also means learning the music behind the guitar, but it's an intuitive process that won't leave you swamped or feeling overwhelmed - which is the case with other instruments.

Now, in all of my time working with people and teaching them to play music, I've heard a lot of different things. Many people have said, for example, that for one reason or another they simply can't make music. "I've tried!", they'd say - "I'm just not cut out for it!" Or that old classic "I don't have any musical talent"

The truth is that anybody *can* make music! It just takes the right approach. It's unfortunate, but a lot of people approach guitar teaching in the wrong way. Many people will come out of it knowing a lot of basic chords on a guitar or perhaps even note names, but they won't really know anything about what they're *doing*. This book changes that paradigm up a little, because let's be honest, I don't think you bought a guitar to spend hours studying sheet music - you just want to get on and play

So here's the situation: you picked up this book because you want to be a fantastic guitar player. That's great! I think that over the course of this book, you'll become an excellent one. In fact, I'll say even more: I think that within just 10 days, and proper dedication, you can become a very proficient guitar player in that amount of time with a bright future of tearing up the fretboard.

So there's my goal in writing this book: create a book which supplies you with all of the knowledge that you need to not only play the guitar, but play it well and play it fast.

Music is something truly incredible. Music has been one of people's primary forms of expression since civilization has existed, and every civilization has had music in one capacity or another. The reason that we love music and art so much is because it links us intrinsically to both culture and emotion, and there is nothing more human than culture and emotion; there is nothing so incredibly valuable.

So when you're learning to play music, you aren't just learning to play music. You're learning to tell people exactly what you're feeling through your expression - after all, music is just a form of expression. And though you may start off with awkward sounding chords and some classic rock covers, as you push more and more, you're going to find that you become a better player as you go - and as such, start creating some cool stuff on your own. Indeed, that's my goal for you!

In the end, what you need to remember is that learning an instrument can be difficult. This is true of anything, but especially instruments because there's no sense of instant gratification. Let's say, for example, that you wanted to start writing poetry, so you started to write poems every single day. The first day, you'd at least be *able* to write a poem, even if it wasn't great, then when you looked back in a month, you would find that your writing had improved quite a bit over the course of the month because you were practicing different concepts and tones of voice every single day.

However, with instruments, you don't have this as much. You still have a linear sense of progression, but you aren't going to have that same degree of immediate gratification that you would get from other pursuits.

But, this isn't necessarily a bad thing, because if you stick it out, you *will* get extremely gratifying results, and I'd argue that they're more gratifying because you ended up waiting for them. In the end, they may just be more gratifying because you like music more than anything else and finally being able to play music will be the greatest thing ever for you.

And also, some people will pick things up faster than others. Again there is no singular path for becoming a great musician. However, this book does have what is optimally a 10 day path. Some people will master the concepts in this book in four or five days, and some will master the concepts in twenty. The average person can get this book down in roughly 10, and that will leave you at a comfortably proficient level in terms of your learning.

THE GUITAR PARTS AND TUNING

*B*efore you start jamming out, you'll need to know the basics of what makes up your guitar itself. In this chapter, we're going to be dissecting the instrument a bit and talking about all of the different parts of the guitar. We're also going to be discussing how you should tune your guitar in order to play most songs, referred to as *standard tuning*.

So let's start from the beginning. Take a look at your guitar, maybe you've had to dig it out from the attic, or maybe it was a brand spanking new birthday or holiday gift from a loved one. Hold it up, and marvel at its beauty.

Your guitar has essentially two basic components: a body and a neck. This book is going to focus exclusively on acoustic guitars, so we're going to be talking about those. However, do note that the things which you learn in this book will also apply to electric guitars.

Anyhow, the body of the acoustic guitar consists of the large part of the body. On many acoustic guitars, this is pear-shaped - these guitars are called *dreadnought* acoustic guitars. However, some acoustic guitars have a section taken out in order to allow players to access the higher frets - these are called *cutaway* acoustic guitars. Both are functionally the same, however - so don't worry about this too much for now

The body has many different parts. The first and most noticeable is the gigantic hole in the body. This is called the *sound hole*. This is the crux of the acoustic guitar. Where electric guitars are plugged into an amplifier (and some acoustic guitars may be as well), most acoustics make sound by way of resonance. This means that the sound waves made by the strings will actually enter the body of the guitar through the sound hole, bounce around, and come back out much louder than they were before.

Right below the sound hole, on many guitars, is a piece of plastic which is glued to the body. This is called the pickguard. This mainly serves a stylistic purpose on the acoustic guitar (most of the time, it doesn't actually *guard* anything).

Next, you have the strings, obviously. We'll be talking more about the strings in the next chapter. There are six of them, and they range from the thickest string which produces the deepest tones to the thinnest string which produces the highest tones.

If you follow the strings to their point of origin, you'll land at the bridge. The bridge is the piece of wood glued to the guitar that's raised up slightly. The bridge has a few different components which make them up.

Firstly, the bridge has little holes drilled in it. Through these holes, you can put your strings. You'll then fix the strings in place with something called a *bridge pin*. These are the small pins that you can see near the bottom of the bridge.

If you look just above this point, you'll see a piece of wood that seems a little arbitrary, holding the strings up. This is called the bridge saddle. This is an important component to a stringed instrument because it raises the strings up enough for the fretted notes to be accurate and to ensure a

GUITAR FOR BEGINNERS

proper proximity from the sound hole which will improve and bolster the quality of the sound.

These are the primary components of an acoustic body. Some acoustic guitars are acoustic-electric. This means that they either have a small microphone built into the sound hole, or they have what are essentially magnets called *pickups* built into the sound hole; either way, the point is allowing the sound to be picked up and sent through an analog signal to a pre-amp. If you're working with an acoustic-electric guitar, then generally the pre-amp will be on the side facing you.

Here, you can make all kinds of changes to the transmitted sound of your guitar, like changing the equalization settings in order to make the sound bassier or have more treble. These kind of guitars will also have an input where you can connect an instrument cable which will then go out to an amplifier.

Now, we must focus on the neck. The neck is the other part of the guitar. The most noticeable part of the neck is the fretboard; this also is the part which takes up the most space. The strings run along the fretboard, where they are divided into individual notes by metal spacers. These spacers indicate to you which note will be played when you press down. Understanding this is an important first step in learning to play the guitar.

The frets often will have some kind of indicator to help you easily find which fret you're on, usually on the third, fifth, seventh, ninth, twelfth, fifteenth, seventeenth, and nineteenth frets. Often, these are simple dots, but they can have many other cool designs as well, and some guitars have no such indicators at all.

Following the neck up further will bring you to a little piece of wood through which the strings are guided. This is called the *nut*. The *nut* is important because it makes sure the strings stay in place as they had up to the part where they are tuned and helps to ensure an equal distance between all strings.

The strings then make their way up to what are called the tuning pegs. They wind through these and are bound around them by the metal things called the *tuners* on the side of the guitar, also sometimes plastic. All of this is taking place on what is called the *headstock*, which just refers to everything on the guitar over the nut. The headstock usually will also have a brand name or a logo.

A guitar, as I said, has six strings. The thickest is called the sixth string while the thinnest is called the first string. The string numbers then run accordingly to this. For example, the second-thinnest string is called the second string, while the second-thickest string is called the fifth string.

It's imperative that you tune your guitar correctly while you're starting out. As you go on, you'll find there are many different ways to tune your guitar; however, there is one *standard* way to tune your guitar, appropriately called standard tuning. The strings in standard tuning are like so:

- The sixth string is tuned to the note E2
- The fifth string is tuned to the note A2
- The fourth string is tuned to the note D3
- The third string is tuned to the note G3
- The fourth string is tuned to the note B3
- The sixth string is tuned to the note E4

The numbers refer to the octave that the note is in on an 81 key piano, starting from the bottom. This doesn't quite make sense to you, and it's something we're going to be discussing a bit more in the following chapter, so don't worry.

An easy way to tune your guitar is to use the fifth fret

method. What you do is you tune the low E string to the appropriate note, E2, then from there, you tune the A string to the fifth fret of the tuned E string. Follow up tuning the D string to the fifth fret of the low A string and so forth, not changing aside from tuning the B string to the *fourth fret* of the tuned G string. While this won't give you automatically perfect tuning, it's a great approximation without pulling out something like a guitar tuner and will get you within 99% accuracy assuming that your musical ear is solid.

Your musical ear, for the record, is something we're going to be talking about a little bit later in the book, so don't worry about that right now.

If you've not sure if you tuned your guitar correctly - then check out this handy YouTube video. It plays each note multiple times so you don't have to stop and start like other tuning videos. http://bit.ly/TuningByEar

BUYING A GUITAR AND STRINGING IT

Buying a guitar is a big decision and will make a big impact on your overall guitar-learning process. There are a lot of different factors which account into buying one that many people don't consider.

First, should you buy a guitar online? No, I'd generally recommend against buying your first guitar online. One of the biggest factors that will keep you coming back to your guitar over and over is whether or not it feels good to you to play it. At first, no matter what guitar you have, it's going to hurt a little bit when you play. However, a huge component of you coming back and practicing more and not mentally avoiding it is how quickly your fingers are able to adapt to your guitar.

What I mean by this is that you should go to local music stores and try to find a guitar that feels good to you. There are many variances in guitar size that can affect how they feel overall, as well as various other changes - such as wood type - that may affect your sound later on but that mean very little when you're starting out.

How will you know when a guitar feels good? Well, there

are a few metrics. First, you need to put your arm all the way down to the first fret, or the first little notch, and hold it appropriately. In order to hold a guitar, what you do is you put it on your right knee (if you're right-handed), then naturally let your body contour to the shape. If it feels like your arm is stretching to reach the first fret, you need to try another guitar, this one is too big and will feel uncomfortable to play.

Another thing you can do in order to determine how comfortable and good of a fit a guitar is is put your index finger on the thinnest string and your thumb on the thickest string, wrapping your hand around the neck. If it feels like your hand has to stretch enough that it hurts, then you need to pick up another guitar. This is a good indicator that the guitar is going to be uncomfortable for long-term advanced play. Your hand will naturally stretch a little bit over time, but not a considerable enough amount for this metric to really change.

Be wary of cheaper guitars. There are many guitars made of cheaper material that are less than $100 which have questionable sound quality, don't hold their tune very well, and are essentially toy guitars. If this is your first guitar, I wouldn't worry too much because it's unlikely you'll notice too much of a difference - but as you move forward on your guitar journey, you might want to upgrade to something a little better.

So how much should you be willing to spend on a first guitar? Realistically, your first guitar should be somewhere between two and three hundred dollars. This doesn't mean that you can't spend more, but I wouldn't recommend it. It also doesn't mean that you can't spend less, but I wouldn't recommend that either. The quality of materials will reflect your sound, and if you use a guitar made of extremely cheap materials, then you most likely aren't going to be getting a sound that you're comfortable with. On the other hand, it's not a good idea - unless you have the money lying around to spend - to invest in an expensive and extremely well-made guitar if you aren't confident that you're going to be sticking around with it for the long-term.

If this is the first time you've tried to learn an instrument, or even the first time you've tried to learn a *stringed* instrument, then it is best to get a guitar that is relatively inexpensive but expensive enough that the materials aren't horrible. This is the best way to ensure that your sound is solid enough that you don't get discouraged by it, but also to ensure that your wallet isn't hurting too much from your decision to invest in a new hobby.

One of the most important parts of the guitar is the strings. Actually, I take that back; strings *are* the most important part of a guitar. Strings have a gigantic impact on your sound, as well as the playability of your guitar. Strings can come in different thicknesses known as *gauges*. Higher gauge strings are harder to push down, but they have a thicker and fuller sound. Meanwhile, lower gauge strings are much easier to play, but their sound is far thinner. It's better to learn on lower gauge strings, generally light gauge or perhaps even extra-light.

Anyhow, the importance of changing your strings is paramount. After a while of usage, the sound of your strings will start to become duller as the strings are exposed to oxygen and usage over a long period of time. If you let them go long enough, they may even start to rust. It's a good idea to change your strings every couple of months or so when you're first starting out. As you progress and begin to play more regularly, you can do this as frequently as every month. Either way, make a habit of changing your strings often.

Restringing an acoustic guitar is a simple process. It can

vary depending upon the guitar, but ultimately the steps are pretty much the same.

The first thing that you need to do is take the current strings off. You do this by detuning the string until it's loose enough to come from from the tuning peg. This will take a minute, so be patient. You'll know when it's loose enough to get it free.

Once all of the strings are free, you then have to stick your hand into the sound hole of the guitar and push up on the bridge pegs from below. This can kind of hurt your fingers, so you may wish to use some sort of fabric in order to push up on these pegs instead. One way or another, the bridge pegs will come out and this will let you pull the string out from the hole. Be careful not to push too hard, or the bridge peg will pop out and you may even lose it.

Some cheaper guitars don't have bridge pegs, but this is one of the reasons that I recommend you get a good guitar in the first place: bridge pegs are a nice feature built into acoustic guitars in order to maintain structural integrity and ensure that the strings don't go where they aren't supposed to.

Anyway, on some guitars, the order of the bridge pegs can make a difference, so once you pull a string out, lightly sit the bridge peg back in the hole from which you got it. Don't push it down into it, you'll just have to pull it back out later. It's not particularly *common* that the order of the bridge pegs makes a difference, but it's not totally unheard of either, so it's certainly worth paying attention for just so nothing goes wrong.

Once you have pulled all of the strings out, you can start putting the strings in their appropriate places. Your pack of strings will usually have them in descending order according to gauge size. The thickest gauge is, of course, the first string. Put them in order according to gauge size then put the ball end of the string into the hole. There is a small notch on the string that indicates roughly how deep the string should be inserted, but put it in a little bit deeper than this just for good measure. The string should be in roughly half an inch before you put the peg in in order to hold it in place.

From here, you need to start winding the strings. This is easy enough. On most guitars, there's either a notch on the tuning peg or a small hole that the string can go through. Either way, you need to feed the string through it and try to pull it so that the string is flush and flat. From here, you need to wind the string. It makes the most sense to turn the tuning peg in the upward direction, or counterclockwise.

When you turn a tuning peg, you're either making the note higher or lower - or, in musical terms, sharper or flatter. This is happening because you are making the string more or less tense when you tune it by winding it either tighter or looser.

The end goal is to have the strings, when they aren't being pressed down, to be the same as the notes which were intimated earlier.

UNDERSTANDING MUSIC NOTES AND TABLATURE

It's important as a guitar student that you're willing to learn the basics of music. Fortunately, the flow of the guitar is simple enough that it tends to leave you with relatively few questions in this department. In that, I mean that you tend to move at a steady enough pace that you don't learn way too much at once and overload yourself.

However, before you even start, there are some basic things that you need to know about music. The first comes down to notes. All of music is broken into a repeating sequence of 11 notes. Note that this isn't always the case; after all, sound can be understood in many different ways, as it's all just a reflection of sonic wavelengths.

But, the Western music tradition does have a way of dividing music that breaks it up into 11 individual semitones. Semitone are the smallest intervals in Western music, and can be measured by keys on a piano. So a semitone is the smallest distance between two keys. Between these semitones lie seven particular notes. We name these notes after the alphabet.

The full 11 notes are like so:

C, C#/Db, D, D#/Eb, E, F, F#/Gb, G, A#/Bb, B

And then the cycle repeats. Most music is just based upon these notes.

The # and *b* are just ways of indicating that the note is either sharp or flat, respectively, which means that it's a semitone higher or lower than the pure note. Notice that B and E don't have sharp variants; they just go directly to the next note up. The reason for this is because the primary way of laying notes out in this manner starts, largely at keyed instruments which were broken up in such a way.

Guitar may be understood through musical notation. However, given all of the different notational nuances to a guitar and the extreme flurry of different notes that it can actually produce, this can be a bizarre and inappropriate way of breaking it down.

That isn't to say that musical notation isn't used; it's used rather often for jazz and classical pieces. However, for everyday music, tablature is generally preferred. This isn't to say that you shouldn't learn to read music; learning to read music is extremely important if you want to be a good musician. I know there are stories out there about people who couldn't read music and became super famous or whatever, like Hendrix, but for the general player - reading music is important if you want to progress.

Not everyone can be the next Hendrix. However, one can easily learn the amount of musical nuance they need in order to be taken seriously by learning the fundamentals, and an important part of learning the fundamentals involves learning to read music notation.

Tablatures

So how does one read tabs? Well, it's pretty simple. There's a little bit of nuance and a learning curve to it, but after you pick it up, it's extremely easy.

Tablatures just take all of the guitar strings and break

them down. They then tell you which notes to play, not by the note but by the fret. This means they tell you which notch to press down on which string.

So what do you lose by learning tabs instead of notes? You lose a little bit of the specificity that music notation offers. Music notation can be a lot more precise than tablature can, by its very nature. **However, the real question is whether or not this matters for the majority of music - and it doesn't.**

More than that, guitar is by-and-large a feel-based instrument. What I mean by this is that the rhythm of a guitar piece can often be felt out just by listening and not by following music to a precise degree, and attempting to play a guitar in a robotic and precise way can make you sound like you're not a confident player.

We aren't going to spend a lot of time in this book going over various exercises to help you read musical notation, because as a beginner guitar student, you don't particularly need it. However, we are going to go over how to read tablature.

Tablature is broken down by the string, and generally has the following layout:

```
e |-----------|
B |-----------|
G |-----------|
D |-----------|
A |-----------|
E |-----------|
```

Note that the thinnest string is on the top where the thickest string is on the bottom.

This is an important distinction. Pay attention to this because if you don't, your music will sound very, very wrong!

The tablature will always indicate what fret you are supposed to play, and the measures will be indicated by the vertical lines. If you don't know much about music, a measure is the way that music is divided into individual parts. There are, generally, four beats to a measure, but some songs have three beats to a measure and some songs have even weirder time signatures. The most common are three or four beats per measure, though.

Here is an example of a basic melody in tablature:

```
e |-----------|-----------|-------|
B |-----------|-----------|-------|
G |-----------|-----------|-------|
D |-----------|-----------|-------|
A |-----------|-----------|-------|
E |---3---2---|---0---2---|---3---|
```

Tablature will also often indicate note lengths. They'll do so using *q*, *h*, *e*, or *w*, as well as other abbreviations. These mean *quarter*, *half*, *eighth*, or *whole note* respectively. These refer to how many beats per measure a note gets. As a beginner, you won't run into many songs with notes smaller than eighth notes.

A quarter note gets a single beat. A half note gets two beats. A whole note gets four beats. An eighth note gets half of a beat.

Here is that same tablature again, but with note lengths:

```
e |-----------|-----------|-------|
B |-----------|-----------|-------|
G |-----------|-----------|-------|
D |-----------|-----------|-------|
A |-----------|-----------|-------|
E |---3---2---|---0---2---|---3---|
```
hh h hw

Tablature will also have little abbreviations which refer to concepts which are even more difficult than those we've already covered. For example, often, if you bend a note up to a new pitch, it'll be intimated with a *b*:

GUITAR FOR BEGINNERS

```
e |-----------|
B |-----------|
G |-----------|
D |-----------|
A |-----------|
E |---7b9-----|
```

Hammer-ons and pull-offs, or when you play one note and then put a finger down or take one off in order to play another note without strumming again, are intimated with an *h*:

```
e |-----------|
B |-----------|
G |-----------|
D |-----------|
A |-----------|
E |---7h9h7---|
```

Muted notes are indicated through the usage of an *x*; a muted note just indicates that a certain note isn't being played in the chord even though you may be strumming fully.

Another thing to take into account in your playing is strum patterns. Strum patterns are really easy to understand but can be a confusing concept at first. Essentially, every song has a certain way in which it's played. This particular rhythm is usually repeated throughout the entire song. This is denoted through a series of upstrums - playing the strings from the first string up - and downstrums - playing the strings from the sixth string down. The exact rhythm of these can massively impact the overall feel and sound of a given guitar composition.

Strum patterns are extremely prevalent on acoustic guitar, which is primarily a rhythm instrument rather than a lead instrument, so having an intimate knowledge of how they work is important. Unfortunately, tablature tends to not divulge too much information on strum patterns. Much of this must be felt out from listening to the song itself.

Now, the cool thing about the guitar is that it has an enormous range. Remember how we talked about notes? The guitar's fretboard actually works in that same semitonal system that we talked about. Here is a chart of the guitar, with notes according to strings and frets up to the 12th fret where they repeat.

0
1
2
3
4
5
6
7
8
9
10
11
12
e
F
F#
G
G#
A
A#
B
C
C#
D
D#
E

B
C
C#
D
D#
E
F
F#
G
G#
A
A#
B
G
G#
A
A#
B
C
C#
D
D#
E
F
F#
G
D
D#
E
F
F#
G
G#
A

A#
B
C
C#
D
A
A#
B
C
C#
D
D#
E
F
F#
G
G#
A
E
F
F#
G
G#
A
A#
B
C
C#
D
D#
E

Remember looking at this that every sharp of a note can also be the flat of the note higher. While musically, there is a small differentiation between the two, it makes little effect on something like a guitar. Feel free to refer back to this chart at later parts in the book when you're working on things such as barre chords, because you'll inevitably find it useful. There is a rhythm to the whole thing that you start to develop naturally after a while.

BASIC MAJOR AND MINOR CHORDS

In this chapter, we're going to be going over basic chord shapes. There are five main chords that you absolutely need to know, so we're going to be going over those first. You need to be reading these chord charts in the same way that you would read tablature. The *p*, *i*, *r*, and *m* just indicate which fingers are used (pinky, index, ring, and middle, respectively) - a zero indicates an open string.

REGARDING HAND POSITIONING, you want to place your fingers on the fret on the side closer to you, against but not on the metal strip. So not in the middle of the fret, but pressed against the side of the metal strip. This reduces the "buzzing" sound you may experience if you play in the middle of the fret.

The first 5 chords

IT MAY SURPRISE YOU, but with just these 5 chords, you can play hundreds of well known songs. Heck, even with just the

GUITAR FOR BEGINNERS

first 3 there are a number of well known tunes that only use G, C and D.

THE FIRST CHORD is G major, which can be played like this:

G major
```
e |---3-------| p
B |---0-------|
G |---0-------|
D |---0-------|
A |---2-------| i
E |---3-------| m
```

THE SECOND CHORD is C major, which can be played like this:

C major
```
e |---0-------|
B |---1-------| i
G |---0-------|
D |---2-------| m
A |---3-------| r
E |---x-------|
```

THE THIRD MAJOR chord is D major, which can be played like this:

D major
```
e |---2-------| i
```

```
B |---3-------| r
G |---2-------| m
D |---0-------|
A |---x-------|
E |---x-------|
```

THE FOURTH IMPORTANT chord is A minor, which can be played like this:

A minor
```
e |---0-------|
B |---1-------| i
G |---2-------| r
D |---2-------| m
A |---0-------|
E |---x-------|
```

THE FIFTH AND final important chord is E minor, which can be played like this:

E minor
```
e |---0-------|
B |---0-------|
G |---0-------|
D |---2-------| r
A |---2-------| m
E |---0-------|
```

THERE ARE many more important chords, and we're going to

be going over those as well, but this are the most important to know as a beginner. Why? Because as a beginner, by using these chords you will be able to play most simple songs. There are a huge number of songs which can be played using only these chords. The majority of folk songs, for example, are based around these chords as well as F and D minor.

WHEN YOU'RE REFERRING to a major chord, you normally don't say major in the name. For example, instead of saying C major, you would simply say "C". However, as a new guitar learner, it's important that you say major in order to learn the distinction between these chords and their minor counterparts.

SO WHAT IS the difference between a minor and a major chord? Well, from a musical standpoint, there's one small difference that can completely change the meaning and tone of the chord: the *third*. The *third* is an important interval in music because it can really impact the overall sound of a chord. The *perfect third* is the note which is three full tones apart from the root, which is the note that the chord is based around. Major chords have a *perfect third*, where minor chords have a *flat third*.

HOWEVER, in layman's terms, the basic difference between minor and major chords is that minor chords sound depressing where major chords sound joyful.

THIS IS an arbitrary and classical distinction, though, and doesn't really apply to modern music where the horizons have been massively expanded due to the last century of pop experimentation. For example, *In My Life* by the Beatles is a sad-sounding song that is written in a major key, where a lot of rock songs are more cheerful and uplifting while being written in a minor key. (This is due largely to the usage of the pentatonic scale in rock and the heavier sound of the minor key, but I could write a whole other book about that subject.)

ANYWAY, the reason I differentiate between the two in a musical aspect is because you're going to find that in order to form a minor chord from a major chord, you are usually just moving one finger. The fret that you are changing is a shift from a perfect third to a minor third.

THIS IS important for you as a new guitar learner because knowing this distinction will help you with connecting the early dots of guitar learning.

NOW, we're going to talk about more open chords that you really need to know as a beginner guitar player. Hopefully, we're going to cover all of the major open chords that you are going to need as you keep pushing forward on your continuing journey to become a masterful guitarist.

D minor
```
e |---1-------| i
B |---3-------| r
G |---2-------| m
D |---0-------|
A |---x-------|
```

```
E |---x-------|
```

A major

```
e |---0-------|
B |---2-------| r
G |---2-------| m
D |---2-------| i
A |---0-------|
E |---x-------|
```

E major

```
e |---0-------|
B |---0-------|
G |---1-------| i
D |---2-------| r
A |---2-------| m
E |---0-------|
```

F major (not an open chord, but still important)

```
e |---1-------| i
B |---1-------| i
G |---2-------| m
D |---3-------| p
A |---3-------| r
E |---x-------|
```

USING THESE CHORD, you're now able to play a huge number of different songs which rely upon open chords - which, coincidentally, is most songs. You can practice switching between the different songs too, if you'd like.

There's yet another chord type that we really need to talk about in this book, and those are barre chords. Barre chords are chords which take open chord shapes and then move them all over the guitar neck. The cool thing about barre chords is that they correspond to the different root notes on the guitar. For example, if you wanted to play an F as a barre chord, you would just take the shape of the open E chord and play it on the first fret. It's really cool!

These aren't something to jump into on day one, and they'll be incredibly frustrating to you, especially if you're trying to learn to play on an acoustic. However, they are without a doubt an important part to introduce into your practice regimen and practicing them in the first several days is the absolute best way to build skill with them, so don't hesitate to start using them as soon as you feel confident with other chords. The cool thing about barre chords is that they literally allow you to play any chord you want, once you have perfected working with them. The hard thing about them is that you have to press an entire fret down with one finger!

Here is the shape of an E-shape barre chord on the second fret, which would be an F# major. To do this, you have to press the second fret down with your index finger, like a metal bar across it:

F# major
```
e |---2-------| i
B |---2-------| i
```

```
G |---3-------| m
D |---4-------| p
A |---4-------| r
E |---2-------| i
```

AND HERE IS the shape of an A-shape barre chord on the second fret, which would be a B major:

B major
```
e |---2-------| i
B |---4-------| m
G |---4-------| p
D |---4-------| r
A |---2-------| i
E |---x-------|
```

NOW THAT WE'RE talking about barre chords, there's one more really important one that we need to talk about: B minor. B minor is important because it's extremely common. F# minor is as well. You'll notice that both B minor and F# minor are just barred versions of their open chord counterparts:

B minor
```
e |---2-------| i
B |---3-------| m
G |---4-------| p
D |---4-------| r
A |---2-------| i
E |---x-------|
```

F# minor
```
e |---2-------| i
B |---2-------| i
G |---2-------| i
D |---4-------| m
A |---4-------| r
E |---2-------| i
```

THE LAST KIND of chord that we're going to talk about is easy: 7th chords. 7th chords, musically, are actually called *dominant 7ths*, and this is because they have a natural seventh in the chord. There are a few different ones that you need to know, and they usually involve a small change to a given root chord:

E7
```
e |---0-------|
B |---0-------|
G |---1-------| i
D |---0-------|
A |---2-------| m
E |---0-------|
```

A7
```
e |---0-------|
B |---2-------| r
G |---0-------|
D |---2-------| m
A |---0-------|
```

```
E |---x-------|
```

D7
```
e |---2-------| r
B |---1-------| i
G |---2-------| m
D |---0-------|
A |---x-------|
E |---x-------|
```

C7
```
e |---0-------|
B |---1-------| i
G |---3-------| p
D |---2-------| m
A |---3-------| r
E |---x-------|
```

G7
```
e |---1-------| i
B |---0-------|
G |---0-------|
D |---0-------|
A |---2-------| m
E |---3-------| r
```

So at one point or another, unless you're just reading straight through the book, then you've probably tried playing a chord or two from this book. You should be, if you're trying to learn to play guitar fast! But, you may have found that it didn't sound exactly like you wanted. Here are some of the biggest mistakes that I run into when I'm working with new guitar players that can put a damper on their sound:

- Check your finger positioning. If your chords aren't coming out crisp and clear, it's possible that you're accidentally muting some strings that you aren't meaning to. How do you check for this? Just look at your fingers. If you're touching any strings other than the ones you are supposed to, just adjust your hand. It's a straightforward process but makes a big difference. It's really easy, as a new guitar player, to play with too relaxed of a hand position, which can then inadvertently lead to you playing poorly altogether. You don't need an extremely stiff grip either as doing that will just lead to you inadvertently killing your fingers, but you need to have some kind of authoritative grip and confidence on the strings you're fretting.

- The second mistake goes somewhat hand-in-hand with the last: ensure that you're pressing down the strings with the proper pressure. It's really easy to press down either too much or too little. If you press down too much, then your tone is actually going to go sharp, which isn't a good thing; this will lead to notes being too high, and this will make you sound bad altogether. However, do note, too, that you can really easily not press *hard enough*. If you do this, the notes will be muted, and no sound will come out. This can be really difficult to make better at first because you haven't quite developed the finger strength that you need in order to play chords consistently, especially on an acoustic. However, just stick with it and you'll start to get better.

Your fingers are going to hurt after you play guitar, for a while. You aren't used to pressing strings down, most of the time, so you're going to have to build proper resistances to doing so. These resistances are called calluses, and they're the natural result of using your fingers constantly. Your fingertips become much rougher and stiffer; it's the same effect that women who sew by hand will often experience on their sewing hand because of accidental pricking. You can develop calluses faster by dipping your fingers in rubbing alcohol after every practice.

The next thing that we need to talk about is chord changes.

Learning to play chord changes is extremely important. Chord changes are the crux of all music. Fluid and fast chord changes are therefore the key to being a good acoustic guitarist. So how, then, can one train their ability to make rapid chord changes? The process is simple: *practicing* chord changes.

The best way to practice chord changes is to find a metronome online and set it to a relatively slow tempo. You can go to onlinemetronome.com - or Google actually has one set up if you type in "online metronome". Practice strumming quarter notes of chords. Do whatever it takes to be ready for the next measure, even if you have to skip the fourth or even third beat of the current measure. Keep doing this until you are proficient at your given tempo, then move up.

Eventually, you can incorporate strum patterns into this mix. This is a great way to build up your skill as a rhythm guitarist from the get-go; however, you may not be terribly creative with strum patterns when you're starting out, so do this at your own discretion. Learning new strum patterns will come naturally as you work with more and more music and start to have a better understanding of how everything works rhythmically.

Which chord changes to practice

You'll be a little lost at first about what chord changes to practice, and the truth is that there is no right answer. Depending on the style of music, chord changes can be almost random, seemingly. However, there are many different patterns that they tend to deviate towards. Here are a few of those, so that you can practice switching between these common patterns and becoming a better guitarist:

1. G major, C major, D major, C major
2. F major, C major, G major, C major
3. E major, A major, D major, A major
4. E minor, A minor, C minor, D major

5. C major, A minor, F major, G major

I WOULD RECOMMEND SETTING a metronome to 80 beats per minute then playing through these one at a time, doing what you can to get up to tempo at a decent rate without flubbing between chord changes. The really hard ones will be the ones involving F - the rest are pretty easy to do. However, at any rate, these are legitimate chord changes and aren't far off from what you'd hear in a lot of pop music. Try to become intimately familiar with them and get to a point where you can do them rather flawlessly.

EXAMPLES OF SONGS TO PLAY

In this chapter, we're going to be going over songs that you can learn really easily in order to gain skill rapidly as a guitarist. We're going to start with really basic ones and then move up to more difficult ones.

Mary had a Little Lamb

```
e|----------------------------------|--------------------------------|
B|--------------------------------1-1-|----------------------------|
G|-2-0---0--2--2-2--2--0--0---0--2------|-2--0---0--2--2-2--0--0--2--0----|
D|-----3------------------------------|------3----------------3-|
A|----------------------------------|--------------------------------|
```

38

GUITAR FOR BEGINNERS

```
E|----------------------------------|----------------------
-----------|
```

Old McDonald Had a Farm

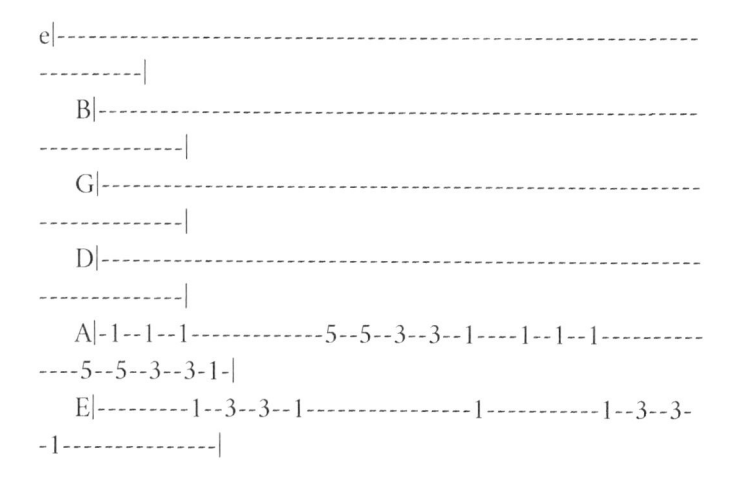

```
e|------------------------------------------------------------
-----------|
   B|---------------------------------------------------------
---------------|
   G|---------------------------------------------------------
---------------|
   D|---------------------------------------------------------
---------------|
   A|-1--1--1-------------5--5--3--3--1----1--1--1----------
----5--5--3--3-1-|
   E|---------1--3--3--1----------------1-----------1--3--3-
-1---------------|
```

Now, we're going to get to playing a few more complicated songs that will really let you practice the chord changes that I'm sure you're itching to work with!

When the Saints Go Marching In

This one is just an American classic. Give it a shot!

C
  Oh when the saints, go marching in.

. . .

G7
> When the saints go marching in.

C F
> I want to be, in that number.

C G7 C
> When the saints go marching in.

AND WHEN THE SUN, refuse to shine.

G7
> And when the sun refuse to shine.

C F
> I still want to be, in that number.

C G7 C
> When the sun refuse to shine.

OH WHEN THE SAINTS, go marching in.

G7
> When the saints go marching in.

GUITAR FOR BEGINNERS

. . .

C F
   I'm gonna to sing, as loud as thunder.

C G7 C
   Oh when the saints go marching in.

C
   Oh when the saints, go marching in.

G7
   When the saints go marching in.

C F
   I want to be, in that number.

C G7 C
   When the saints go marching in.

OH WHEN THE SAINTS, go marching in.

G7
   When the saints go marching in.

C F

I still want to be, in that number.

C G7 C
When the sun refuse to shine.

SILENT NIGHT

CHRISTMAS SONGS ARE great because they're generally pretty easy to learn and play, everybody knows them, and they give you a song you can whip out during the holiday season, too!

G D7 G
Silent Night, Holy Night, all is calm, all is bright,
C G C G
'round yon virgin, mother and child, Holy infant so tender and mild,
D7 G D7 G
sleep in heavenly peace, sleep in heavenly peace.

G D7 G
Silent Night, Holy Night, Shepherds quake, At the sight
C G C G
Glories stream from Heaven above, Heavenly Hosts sing Alleluia,
D7 G G D7 G
Christ the Savior is born, Christ the Savior is born!

G D7 G

GUITAR FOR BEGINNERS

Silent night, Holy night, Son of God, Love's pure light,
C G C G
radiant beams from Thy Holy face, with the dawn of redeeming grace,
D7 G D7 G
Jesus, Lord at Thy birth, Jesus, Lord at Thy birth.

Deck the Hall

This is just another Christmas song. It's great because it lets you practice the D-Bm-A chord progression, which is very common.

D Bm
Deck the hall with boughs of holly,
A7 D D A D
Fa la la la la, la la la la
D Bm
'Tis the season to be jolly.
A7 D D A D
Fa la la la la, la la la la
A7 D
Don we now our gay apparel,
D Bm E7 A
Fa la la la la la, la la la
D Bm
Troll the ancient Yuletide carol.
G D D A7 D
Fa la la la la, la la la la

. . .

LANCE VOIGHT

SEE the blazing Yule before us. Fa la la...
   Strike the harp and join the chorus. Fa la la...
   Follow me in merry measure, Fa la la...
   While I tell the Yuletide treasure. Fa la la...

FAST AWAY THE old year passes, Fa la la la la ...
   Hail the new, ye lads and lasses! Fa la la la la ...
   Sing we joyous all together, Fa la la...
   Heedless of the wind and weather. Fa la la...

RUDOLPH THE RED-NOSED Reindeer

ANOTHER GREAT SONG TO LEARN! This one's really simple but lets you practice more complicated chord changes, like Dm to G7 to C.

C
   Rudolph the red-nosed reindeer,
   G7
   Had a very shiny nose,

AND IF YOU ever saw it,
   C
   You would even say it glows.
   C
   All of the other reindeer,
   G7
   Used to laugh and call him names,

. . .

They never let poor Rudolph,
   C C7
   Join in any reindeer games.
   F C Dm G7 C
   Then one foggy Christmas Eve, Santa came to say,
   G D7 G7
   "Rudolph with your nose so bright, won't you guide my sleigh tonight?"
   C
   Then how the reindeer loved him,
   G7
   As they shouted out with glee,

"Rudolph the red-nosed reindeer,
   C
   You'll go down in history."

Jingle Bells

Everybody knows this song by heart. Prove that you do by learning to play it!

C
   Dashing through the snow
   F
   In a one horse open sleigh
   G
   O'er the fields we go
   C
   Laughing all the way

LANCE VOIGHT

C
Bells on bob tails ring
C7 F
Making spirits bright
F G
What fun it is to laugh and sing
C
A sleighing song tonight

G C
Oh, jingle bells, jingle bells

Jingle all the way
   G7 C
   Oh, what fun it is to ride
   D7 G
   In a one horse open sleigh
   C
   Jingle bells, jingle bells

Jingle all the way
   G7 C
   Oh, what fun it is to ride
   G C
   In a one horse open sleigh

C
A day or two ago,
F
I thought I'd take a ride

G
And soon Miss Fanny Bright,
C
Was seated by my side
C
The horse was lean and lank,
C7 F
Misfortune seemed his lot
G
We got into a drifted bank,
C
And then we got up-sot

G C
   Oh, jingle bells, jingle bells

JINGLE all the way
   G7 C
   Oh, what fun it is to ride
   D7 G
   In a one horse open sleigh
   C
   Jingle bells, jingle bells

JINGLE all the way
   G7 C
   Oh, what fun it is to ride
   G C
   In a one horse open sleigh 2x

                   . . .

Greensleeves

THIS SONG IS fantastic to learn because the melody is familiar, plus the chord progression is extremely common. It's also the only minor key song that we're covering in this chapter.

[VERSE]

Am C
   Alas my love,
G Em
   you do me wrong,
Am E
   to cast me off so discourteously,
Am C G Em
   for i have loved you so long,
Am E7 Am
   delighting in your company.

[Chorus]

C G Em
   greensleeves was all my joy,
Am E
   greensleeves was my delight,
C G Em
   greensleeves was my heart of gold,
Am E7 Am

and who but my lady greensleeves.

[Verse 2]

Am C G Em
    Thy gown was of the grassy green,
Am E
    Thy sleeves of satin hanging by,
Am C G Em
    Which made thee be our harvest queen,
Am E7 Am
    And yet thou wouldst not love me.

[Chorus]

C G Em
    greensleeves was all my joy,
Am E
    greensleeves was my delight,
C G Em
    greensleeves was my heart of gold,
Am E7 Am
    and who but my lady greensleeves.

[Verse 3]

Am C G Em
    Well, i will pray to God on high,

Am E
That thou constancy mayst see,
Am C G Em
And that yet once before i die,
Am E7 Am
Thou will vouchsafe to love me.

STREETS OF LAREDO

THIS ONE IS a classic cowboy hymn. A lot of people know it, and that's for good reason: it's a lot of fun to sing and to play! The chord Bb is unfamiliar, but it's just an A-shape barre chord on the first fret. This is a great way to practice your more complex chord shapes.

F C7 F C7
   As I walked out in the streets of La-re-do, As
F Bb F C7
   I walked out in La-re-do one day, I
F C7 F C7
   spied a young cowboy wrapped up in white linen, wrapped
F Bb F C7 F
   up in white linen and cold as the clay.

"I SEE by your outfit that you are a cowboy." These
   words, he did say as I boldly stepped by. "Come
   sit down be-side me and hear my sad story; I'm
   shot in the breast and I know I must die."

. . .

"Oh, beat the drum slowly and play the fife lowly;
    Play the Dead March as you carry me a-long. Take me
    to the green valley and lay the sod o'er me, For
    I'm a young cowboy and I know I've done wrong."

"It was once in the saddle I used to go dashing;
    It was once in the saddle I used to go gay.
    First to the dram house and then to the card house,
    Got shot in the breast and I'm dying today."

"Get six jolly cowboys to carry my coffin;
    Get six pretty maidens to bear up my pall.
    Put bunches of roses all over my coffin,
    Put roses to deaden the clods as they fall."

"Go bring me a cup, a cup of cold water
    To cool my parched lips," the young cowboy said.
    Before I returned, the spirit had left him
    And gone to its Maker-- the cowboy was dead.

We beat the drum slowly and played the fife lowly,
    And bitterly wept as we bore him along.
    For we all loved our comrade, so brave, young, and handsome,
    We all loved our comrade although he'd done wrong.

Home on the Range

. . .

This one is great because it lets you practice an E-minor barre chord shape, thanks to the G minor. That's just an E-minor barre chord shape on the third fret. Give this one a go!

[Verse]

D G Gm
   Oh give me a home where the buffalo roam,
D E7 A7
   Where the deer and the antelope play.
D G Gm
   Where seldom is heard a discouraging word,
D A7 D
   And the skies are not cloudy all day.

[Chorus]

D A7 D
   Home, home on the range,
Bm E7 A7
   Where the deer and the antelope play.
D G Gm
   Where seldom is heard a discouraging word,
D A7 D
   And the skies are not cloudy all day.

COMMON BEGINNER ISSUES

Your hands hurt

Welcome to the club. Don't worry - this is completely normal. The only way this pain will go away is practice.

Your hands are too small

Now this issue probably isn't an issue at all. Many beginners mistake the hand awkward hand positioning when they first play, with their hands being too small. Remember, these will be hand positions unlike any others you have experienced before. It's like the first time you try and hit a baseball or do yoga - you body isn't used to it.

Your hit the wrong strings

This tends to occur when you pluck 2 non-adjacent strings. It's just a matter of practice, and developing a "feel" for the instrument

You don't have time to practice

I get it , you're busy. Just set aside 30 minutes a day, preferably at the same time each day so that you develop a consistent habit.

Neglecting barre chords

We went over this briefly before, and barre chords can

seem intimidating at first. Because many songs, especially beginner ones don't include them - they tend to get left behind. But you will need them as you progress to the next level, so make sure you dedicate at least 10 minutes a day to barre chords and incorporate songs which use barre chords into your practice routine.

Only practicing chords, and not practicing songs

You didn't buy a guitar so you could just play chords over and over again. You need to put those chords together in the form of songs. In the bonus resource chapter of this book I've included both tabs and YouTube videos for basic songs you can play.

CONCLUSION: BRINGING IT ALL TOGETHER

Thank for making it through to the end of *Learn the Guitar in 10 Days*, let's hope it was informative and able to provide you with all of the tools you need to achieve your goals whatever it may be.

Perhaps the biggest thing that you can focus on right now is focus on training your musical ear. So how do you do that exactly? The most immediate and easy way is to just start playing chords and practicing scales as well. By doing this, you'll build natural musical connections in your brain. And for those of you who say that it doesn't work like that, I'm living proof; when I was young, I couldn't sing at all. However, I joined a choir on a whim and started to train my ability and became a very skillful singer through hard work and dedication, as cliché as that may seem to some people. Work is really the driving factor.

If you work with everything in this book (and music in general) for long enough, you're going to start to feel a very innate and natural understanding of the different concepts at play. Taking this into account, you'll grow a lot as a guitarist

CONCLUSION: BRINGING IT ALL TOGETHER

and a musician in general. Again, though, it's not going to come with a day's work; being a good musician is a constant journey to improve, and every day will ideally teach you something new.

The next step is to just build on all of the things that you learned. There are two primary ways to do this.

The first is to learn more songs. Think about what kind of music specifically interests you. This is a little harder to connect the dots on if you primarily listen to hip-hop, metal, or something of the like, but most other forms of music have very clearly defined chords and melodies. For example, alternative rock, country, classic rock, and post-punk all have valuable lessons that they can teach you on musicality simply by learning their songs.

So what you need to do is find whatever things interest you and then use those in order to push yourself further on the guitar. Your mind will learn new concepts faster because you're doing something that you actively like while you try to push yourself further as a musician.

If you want to be a songwriter, then just start as soon as possible. Start training concepts from the get-go and writing songs because you'll only get better and solidify things. As you saw in the last chapter, hit songs can be written using only a few chords, so it's not like you need a whole lot in order to become a good guitarist.

The second thing that you can do in order to take all of these concepts further is start practicing scales and more complex things. These aren't as applicable on acoustic guitars, but the practice and musicality that you learn from these sorts of

CONCLUSION: BRINGING IT ALL TOGETHER

exercises are still important. In fact, there are a huge number of different acoustic guitarists who are popular specifically for the reason that they have an excellent sense of musicality that can only be obtained through constant practice and work with foreign musical concepts, like Elliott Smith.

In the end, my goal was to write a book that would help you to become a proficient guitarist in a relatively short amount of time. Unfortunately, this also means that the learning curve of this book can be a little bit steep, but it seems that's the price one must pay for wanting to learn something so in-depth so fast. However, hopefully the payoff is such that it doesn't really matter - if you put in the time, this book will reward you, and it's as simple as that.

So in the end, I'd like to wish you the best of luck. I really hope that I succeeded in my goal of making a book that would help you to quickly become a proficient and able guitarist.

As a last note, I'd just like to remind you to stick with it; learning an instrument is *not* easy. Even though I hope that I can make it just a little bit easier by making this book, in the end, there still will be times where you absolutely want to pull your hair out. During these times, just keep going with it! The end result will be quite rewarding, I assure you.

Again, good luck and thank you for reading!

Printed in Great Britain
by Amazon